STOP PROCRASTINATING—DO IT!

STOP PROCRASTINATING—
DO IT!

JAMES R. SHERMAN

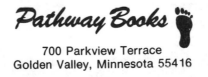

700 Parkview Terrace
Golden Valley, Minnesota 55416

Pathway Books
700 Parkview Terrace
Golden Valley, Minnesota 55416
(612) 377-1521

iv

Refd	1	1901 5
Refd	1	17039
Refd	1	17042
Refd	1	34D38
		Received
		Will

CREDIT SLIP
ON "WHY TRAD
#16040 $7.9
[TOTAL REFUND

To: Roger

CONTENTS

WHY PEOPLE PROCRASTINATE

HOW TO STOP PROCRASTINATING

YOUR PLAN OF ACTION

PREFACE

Here's a book I've wanted to write for a long time. But I just never got around to it.

I've probably procrastinated as much as anybody. And like many other people, I've let a lot of good living go by unattended. But there were times when I really hustled to get something done. Then I learned how to avoid postponements and delays. And I remembered what I'd learned. So each time I faced another important task I knew what I had to do to get it done.

My first try for a college degree ended in failure. I went back later with a wife and three sons and kept going until I had my bachelor's, master's, and Ph.D. To get my doctorate I did all my coursework, conducted research, wrote my dissertation, served several internships, completed all my exams, and commuted over 40,000 miles—all in six consecutive quarters.

Then my wife and I each had three disabling back operations during a five-year period. I hurt all the time and could hardly do anything. But I didn't want to stay that way. So I lost weight, started exercising, and got rid of all my pain and muscle-relaxing pills. Now I play racquetball and golf and am completely free of pain.

Last year I quit a well-paying job as consultant to colleges and universities and started a self-publishing firm. This is my second book.

Through all this I discovered how to stop procrastinating. And I found that it's pretty easy to do. There's nothing new involved. You just apply what's already known. The secret is to understand what you're doing, decide you want something better, and get on with it.

I've combined my experiences with some extensive research into a simple, straightforward method for overcoming procrastination. It's worked for me. I really believe it'll work for you. Just read this book, do what it says, refer to it as needed, and you'll stop procrastinating. Then tell me about your success. I'd enjoy hearing from you.

JAMES R. SHERMAN, Ph.D.

ACKNOWLEDGEMENTS

Thanks to my wife Merlene, my son Chris, Dale Lorenz, and Barbara Baker for their editorial reviews, helpful suggestions, and unfailing support. And thanks also to sons Eric and Lincoln who made this book necessary.

INTRODUCTION

Congratulations! You took your first step toward breaking the habit of procrastination when you picked up this book. Keep going. You could end up making some significant changes in your life. You've got a good start. Now you have to keep your momentum by discovering some things about yourself and this good-for-nothing habit you're trying to get rid of.

You're probably one of several million well-intentioned people who tends to postpone or delay some of the important things you should be doing. That doesn't mean you'll lose all your hair or develop a terminal case of toejam. But it does mean you've been shortchanging yourself out of some of the better things in life.

Like most procrastinators, you know who and what you are, but you want something better. You probably are—or are striving to become a successful executive, a super college student, a first-class homemaker, or the very best of whatever you are. Only you're frustrated because you're unable to do everything you want to do. You postpone things you should be doing and that bothers you.

You know procrastination is a lousy habit that can affect you both mentally and physically by causing stress, tension, anxiety, and fatigue. You also know it can keep you from reaching the goals and objectives you've set for yourself. It can stifle your personal growth and keep you from getting rewards that should be yours. And worst of all, it can keep you from living a happier and healthier life.

Now you're ready to learn more about procrastination and how you can stop doing it. It should be easy for you because you're motivated. You just need a simple, straightforward procedure that will answer your questions and show you how to move ahead.

Here's a method that probably fits the bill.

A METHOD

Carry out these four fundamental steps and you'll stop procrastinating. Just be careful with the first step. It's the hardest one of all for many people because it requires a personal commitment. If you get past it, you'll have smooth sailing with the other three.

1. Admit that you procrastinate and make up your mind to stop doing it.
2. Learn as much as you can about procrastination; what it is, what causes it, and what can be done to stop it.
3. Decide on a definite plan of action. Make a list of specific things you're going to do right away to stop procrastinating.
4. Carry out your plan.

Now stop a minute. Go back to the first step. Are you really serious about putting an end to procrastination? If you're determined to do it, go on to the next section and find out what procrastination is all about. But don't go on until you've made a commitment to change.

A DEFINITION

Procrastination is the intentional and habitual postponement of something that should be done. It can involve some pretty complex behavior. But even then it's not too difficult to understand.

First of all, procrastination involves a specific task that's important for you to do. At least you think it is. It can be going on a diet, writing a letter, proposing marriage, or starting a new career. It can be almost anything in your life with a beginning, an ending, and a definite outcome. You can tell how important it is for you to complete your task by figuring out what would happen if you didn't do it.

Your task should have an obvious conclusion. And everyone involved with it should know what it is. A specific bodyweight will be reached, a document will be produced, a behavioral change will be completed, or some other goal will be accomplished.

You should have a specific day, hour, year, or some other time when your task will be completed. You should know what's early and what's late. "Any old time" is much too vague.

You have to deliberately avoid your task in order to procrastinate. You can do this by playing dead or by substituting other behavior like sleeping, eating, drinking, playing tennis, or doing busy work.

And finally, you have to feel guilty about not doing what you're supposed to do. A little anxiety about goofing off can develop into painful depression if you're really into bigtime procrastination. But generally you'll just sweat a little when you postpone a visit to the dentist or try to avoid your mother-in-law.

The more you know about the causes of procrastination, the easier it'll be to break the habit. You might be tempted to skip the next section if you think you already know why you procrastinate. But even if you think you know most of the reasons, you could be surprised by some others. So take a little time and check out the next section. You'll be glad you did.

WHY PEOPLE PROCRASTINATE

People procrastinate for lots of reasons. Psychologists will probably say it's because they're insecure, afraid of failure, or unable to cope with things that are frustrating, threatening, or go bump in the night. That's pretty strong. But it indicates some of the things that can bring on delays and postponements.

People also procrastinate because of subconscious thoughts. They know they should do something, but they're unable to do it without knowing why. Sometimes it's a subconscious fear that keeps them from taking action.

Many people think they postpone things for reasons that aren't very serious. And they think they can stop procrastinating without having to undergo major behavioral changes. But any reason should be considered serious if it keeps people from enjoying some of the nicer things in life.

If you're like most procrastinators, you're actively concerned about the things you do and you'd like to do better. You recognize and understand some of the major causes of your procrastination, but you find others are hard to identify. If that's true, then this section will help you understand the causes of procrastination. But before you start into it, do this simple exercise.

Take a sheet of paper and write down the reasons why you procrastinate. List as many as you can—at least ten. Then as you go through this section, compare your list with what you find here. You may find more reasons than you have listed. Or you may have some that aren't included here. That's okay. This section includes the most common causes, not necessarily the prizewinners. You'll still get a good understanding of what you're doing by studying the entire section even if some of the causes are missing or if others don't apply. And besides, it'll help you get ready for the last section. That's the one that shows you how to put your desire to stop procrastinating into action.

The causes that follow aren't listed in any particular order of importance. You'll have to determine how important they are after you've studied them and figured out how they affect you. The first one seems to bother an awful lot of people.

CONFUSION

Sometimes people procrastinate because they're confused and uncertain about what to do next. They're usually overwhelmed by the size and complexity of a task. They discover a multitude of parts but they can't decide which one to start on. So they delay and hope their task will somehow shrink to the point where they can see how to get going.

These people know they can proceed by trial and error. But they're so confused they have no idea of what to try. They think they'll screw up no matter what they do. They can cope with their mistakes because they know they can start over again and try something else. They also know restarting takes time. And the size of their task tells them that time is already scarce. All this confusion combines to keep them from making any moves. So they stay put and procrastinate.

People who're confused usually fail to analyze the things they have to do. And that can lead to another cause of procrastination.

ANALYTICAL ABILITY

When people do a poor job of analyzing a task, they usually reject every option that comes to mind. They procrastinate because they're afraid nothing will work. At the same time, they fail to look for possible alternatives. It's like cutting off tree branches before they can bear fruit.

Sometimes these people get themselves trapped. They procrastinate right up to a deadline. Then they scramble to complete a task in the little time that remains. But when they're almost done, they suddenly discover a better solution. If it's too late to start over, they'll wind up with a lousy performance. And they'll wish they'd done things differently. They'll keep procrastinating if this happens a lot because they'll be afraid of making similar mistakes in the future.

Knowing what to do helps get people moving. But knowing what to do first is even more important.

PRIORITIES

Lack of priorities is one of the most common causes of procrastination. People lose their sense of urgency about what things should be done first if they fail to attach priorities to their tasks. They jump from task to task and are unable to get much of anything done.

People also find it difficult to say "no" if they refuse—or are unable—to set priorities. That's because it's hard for them to know what's important and what's not. They give their time and energy to everything that's passed on to them. They end up with too much to do and no organized way of doing it. They keep putting things off, trying to find a way through the mess they've created.

An even bigger mess can develop when people forget what they're supposed to do. But sometimes procrastinators say they forgot when they actually mean something else.

FORGETFULLNESS

If people really forget a task, they won't remember anything about it. They won't even notice the task when it's right in front of them. This can happen sometimes. People can forget. But usually it's a case of subconscious disregard. And that follows a fairly predictable pattern.

First of all, certain tasks should be done as soon as possible and people know that. But instead of being completed, the tasks are intentionally shoved into low-priority corners of the procrastinators' immediate surroundings. They're out of the way, but they can still be reached. When asked if they're done, each procrastinator will say "I completely forgot about it." But those statements are usually false because procrastinators still know the tasks exist somewhere. When casual thoughts bring the tasks into focus, the procrastinators begin to feel uneasy, even though they still appear unconcerned about finishing them. Their general lack of awareness indicates that they've subconsciously disregarded their tasks.

People suddenly discover they're responsible for what they do once they stop ignoring their tasks and start taking action. That scares some of them so much they don't get anything done.

RESPONSIBILITY

Sometimes people procrastinate because they're unwilling to accept more responsibility than they think they already have. Students try to stay in college to keep from going to work. Couples extend their engagements to escape the responsibilities of marriage. Employees turn down promotions to avoid responsibilities that come with advancement. And people with physical ailments prolong their recovery to avoid responsibilities they had when they were healthy.

These people always wait until they think conditions have improved before they take their first step. And they'll rationalize their delays by blaming everyone else for making those conditions intolerable. They'll keep procrastinating until they're willing to grow and assume responsibility for the forces in their environment that affect them.

When these people finally accept responsibility, they recognize that they're going to have to be accountable for their actions, whether right or wrong. But exposing themselves to the chance of being wrong can cause some of them to keep on procrastinating.

RISK

People procrastinate to protect themselves from the risks of change. As long as they avoid taking risks, they'll be unaffected by the unknown. They'll escape the potential consequences of career changes, marriage, or geographical relocation. And they'll get very little done as a result.

Risks can be social, psychological, physical, or economic. And procrastinators will exaggerate them whether they are real or make-believe. So even the slightest risk will seem enormous. And the greater the perceived risk, the longer the delay. There's no way this cause of procrastination can be eliminated until risk is accepted as a natural part of life.

About this time you're probably thinking some of these causes don't relate to you. And you'd like to escape by finding something that's more relevant. Well, hang in there. Because escape is just another cause of procrastination.

ESCAPE

People generally react in one of two ways when they're confronted with an unpleasant task. They either struggle to complete it, or they try to escape. And they almost always use procrastination as their means of escape.

People can be pretty aggressive in completing a task if some sort of threat exists. But aggression isn't universally accepted behavior, especially when other people are involved. People are encouraged instead to reason and compromise with their adversaries. Attack is considered uncivilized unless someone has been threatened with bodily harm. And even then people are often encouraged to turn the other cheek.

Unfortunately, reason, compromise, and negotiation require skills that very few people have. So when everybody else is faced with an unpleasant personal confrontation, they'll either be aggressive or they'll escape by procrastinating.

Sometimes people escape from unpleasant tasks so they can be by themselves to get their thoughts in order. But they can't escape from their deadlines. Their stress, tension, and anxiety will continue to grow until their tasks are completed and the deadlines are gone. So those who've tried to escape must continue to search for ways of finishing their tasks. Otherwise they'll just compound the conditions that made them escape in the first place.

People will start to worry about all the things they have to do if they ignore them for too long. A little worry is okay. But when it gets out of hand, it can lead to the next cause of procrastination.

ANXIETY

Anxiety is a sense of apprehension, fear, or painfullness of mind, usually over an impending or anticipated misfortune. It can be both the cause and effect of procrastination.

Anxious people are generally confused about reality and their ability to deal with it. They get anxious in response to real or imagined threats in their environment. And they procrastinate to avoid dealing with those threats.

The threat of an unhappy personal confrontation is a very common cause of anxiety. Anticipated criticism from others is another common cause that can produce anxiety as a byproduct of people's fear of failure.

Anxiety can also be the byproduct of procrastination. People get anxious when they think about the importance of finishing a task. They know they should be doing something, and their anxiety builds because they're procrastinating instead of acting. In this case, their anxiety is caused by their hesitancy rather than by external factors.

Anxiety is a fairly common condition. Lots of people experience it from time to time in their lives. It usually comes and goes as conditions change. But when anxiety continues for long periods of time, it can easily turn into depression, which is a more serious cause of procrastination.

DEPRESSION

Depression is a neurotic condition, characterized by dejection and despair, in which people feel incapable of doing anything about the things that bother them. It's a condition that very often leads to procrastination. And it's a tough one to overcome.

It's hard for people to make decisions of any kind when they're depressed. They feel totally helpless because they think their destiny is controlled by others. So they neglect most of the things they should be doing.

Depression also brings on psychological fatigue. And many people use that as another excuse for procrastinating. Ironically, one of the best ways for people to escape depression is to participate in some strenuous physical activity that they can control and enjoy. But they're so lethargic they just can't seem to get started in those kinds of activities.

Some people may need professional help from a counselor or psychologist if their depression is severe. But being depressed, they'll probably postpone that too. In spite of its gloomy nature, depression can be eliminated along with the procrastination that goes with it. It's not easy. But it can be done.

Fortunately only a limited number of people procrastinate because of depression. A lot more people are affected by less serious behavioral problems.

OBSESSIVE/COMPULSIVE BEHAVIOR

Obsessive people seek perfection in everything they do. They postpone completion of every task until they're sure the outcome will be perfect. As a result, they accomplish very little even though they're very active. This constant state of doing but not finishing shields them from criticism. If others find fault in their efforts, they can always say they're "still working on it."

Most people accept mistakes as a natural part of growth and development. But obsessive procrastinators see mistakes of any kind as devastating indictments of personal weakness. They keep procrastinating because they're afraid of failing.

Compulsive procrastinators also spend lots of time doing things without getting anything done. They try to create the illusion of being in constant and complete control. They feel compelled to take on an excessive number of tasks, starting new ones before old ones are finished. The hallmark of a compulsive procrastinator is a cluttered desk and a hectic pace. They want other people to think they're very busy. But they're reluctant to finish anything because they're afraid of being criticized. So they continue to procrastinate and add more tasks to those they already have.

Obsessive/compulsive procrastinators tend to be very self-centered. They're almost the opposite of people who must always turn to others for help in getting anything done.

DEPENDENCE ON OTHERS

Dependent people procrastinate because they're unable to do things for themselves. They postpone significant tasks until someone helps them or does the tasks for them. They're almost totally dependent upon the skill, strength, or knowledge of others. Sometimes they'll readily admit their dependence. But in most cases they'll deny it.

Finding examples of this kind of procrastination is easy because it's so widespread. Executives will postpone important letters or reports until their favorite secretaries return from vacation. Quarterbacks hesitate to call previously successful plays if regular players are sidelined with injuries. Fathers and mothers wait to discipline their children until the other spouse is present.

Procrastinators will develop a regular pattern of dependent behavior if they're successful in getting help from others. And they'll use it as long as it pays off. They'll quit procrastinating only when they see the advantages of independence and develop a desire to do things for themselves.

Dependent people turn to others because they feel they're unable to fend for themselves. There's another group of people who turn to others as a means of gaining a personal advantage. Their procrastination is caused by a deliberate attempt to use other people.

MANIPULATION OF OTHERS

If other people are involved in important tasks that procrastinators are supposed to be doing, they'll get impatient when those tasks are left undone. And if procrastinators know how the others feel, they'll keep delaying until the others offer to help. It's an effective way for procrastinators to avoid a task or to escape responsibility for the end result.

People will generally avoid being manipulated as much as possible. But they'll get taken in whenever a procrastinator can recognize and pull off an opportunity to do so. And strangely enough, if an important task is at stake, other people will still help the procrastinator even when they don't want to. When help is finally refused, the procrastinator will go in search of another pigeon.

Children are usually very good at manipulating people, especially their parents. But it's inappropriate for adults to continue this childish behavior. It not only leads to procrastination, it's also unfair to other people.

Sometimes the shoe is on the other foot and the procrastinator is the one who's manipulated. Pressure from other people can be a common cause of procrastination even if it's unintentional.

EXTERNAL PRESSURES

Most people know why they procrastinate. It's generally due to conditions they bring on themselves. They can usually stop procrastinating if they work hard to control those conditions. But it will be a lot harder for them if their delays are caused by external pressures they can't control.

Pressure can come from parents, employers, roommates, or spouses. It can very easily steer people in directions they would rather avoid. Employees postpone vacations because their employers want them to work. Women postpone career changes if their husbands withhold support. And couples postpone marriage in the face of parental opposition.

Pressure can be applied over long periods of time. And it can be of a social, psychological, physical, or economic nature.

People will have a hard time taking command of their behavior as long as they let external pressures control them. They'll continue to procrastinate until they're able to identify the sources of pressure, devise ways of regaining control, and begin doing things entirely on their own.

There are only four more reasons in this section. So don't quit now even if you think it's starting to get monotonous. Because that's the next cause.

MONOTONY

Many people will procrastinate when they're faced with a very monotonous task. And they'll continue to procrastinate until the fundamental characteristics of the task are changed.

A task is monotonous if it's tedius, uninteresting, lacks variety, and offers no incentives or rewards. If it's a lousy task, people will continue to think it's monotonous until something is done to change it.

Sometimes people think a task is monotonous when it's not. This is especially true when the people doing it don't understand why it should be done. Then their perception of the task needs to be changed if it's going to be finished. They have to recognize and accept the interesting characteristics that are inherent in the task. And they have to see the benefits that can come from its completion.

If people fail to see any benefits in a task they may be looking at another cause of procrastination.

BOREDOM

Boredom is a common psychological reaction that often leads to procrastination. Unlike monotony, boredom is due to a person's reactions, not the inherent characteristics of a task.

People are weary and dissatisfied when they're bored. They take no interest in the things they're supposed to be doing. They frequently suffer psychological fatigue. And they often use their subjective states of exhaustion as excuses for procrastinating.

Tasks can be changed to make them more interesting. But the main problem in overcoming boredom lies in changing the attitudes of the procrastinators.

Enthusiasm and energy can help relieve boredom. But when they're missing, another cause of procrastination can be introduced.

FATIGUE

Physical and psychological fatigue are both major causes of procrastination. Physical fatigue comes from hard labor, overexertion, or nervous exhaustion. People are usually still interested in completing their tasks when they're physically fatigued. But they lack the energy needed to continue. They procrastinate because they're tired.

Psychological fatigue shows many of the same symptoms like exhaustion, weariness, and lack of energy. But psychological fatigue comes from boredom, apathy, and lack of interest, not from working too hard.

The difference between the two is especially important when people want to stop procrastinating. Physical fatigue calls for rest. Psychological fatigue requires rest and a change in motivation toward the task.

Fatigue is only one of many health-related causes of procrastination. There are others that can not only bring about delays and postponements but a lot of confusion as well.

PHYSICAL DISABILITIES

People procrastinate when they think they're physically incapable of doing something that should be done. Bad backs, poor eyesight, lack of strength, injuries, or illnesses can all be used as reasons for postponement. And delays will continue until the physical disabilities are gone.

People compound their procrastination when they fail to correct their disabilities. They'll delay an automobile trip because of poor eyesight and postpone a visit to an optometrist for a new prescription. Or they'll avoid physical labor because of back pain and also put off going to a doctor for treatment.

Most procrastinators experience anxiety when physical disabilities keep them idle. Not so with people who are malingerers. They only pretend to feel that way. They deliberately use real or imagined disabilities as reasons for avoiding work or responsibilities of any kind. They feel absolutely no remorse or anxiety about their behavior. And they have neither the intention nor the desire to eliminate their disabilities as long as personal benefits can be realized.

There's a big difference between malingerers and people who procrastinate because of physical disabilities. Malingerers feel as though they've done nothing wrong. Procrastinators feel bad about putting things off and they wish they knew how they could change.

Physical disabilities is the last in this list of common causes of procrastination. Now it's time to summarize and look at what's ahead.

TRANSITION

You've seen why many people procrastinate. And you probably found some of the things you had listed when you read through the causes that were presented here. The comparison between your list and this list probably helped even if your behavior is slightly different. Because now you know you're like lots of other people who have trouble with postponements and delays. You've started to analyze your behavior. And that's a very big step forward.

The next section contains a number of suggestions that will help you stop procrastinating. Match those you think will work best against the causes that bother you most. Learn how to conquer your fears if fear causes you to procrastinate. Boost your ego if you're depressed. Subdivide if complex tasks frustrate you. And if you come up with suggestions that aren't in the next section, go ahead and use them whenever you can.

You'll experience the satisfaction of getting things done as you work through the causes and cures. You'll gain momentum as you go along. And you'll start having fun and enjoying yourself. Procrastination will be a thing of the past before you know it. So start now with section three and learn how you can have a more satisfying and rewarding life.

HOW TO STOP PROCRASTINATING

The best time to stop procrastinating is right now. Start by thinking of all the important things you've been postponing—the letters and reports you should have written, the phone calls you should have made, or the book you should have read. Write them all down on a sheet of paper.

Then get out your list of reasons for procrastinating that you made at the beginning of the last section. Compare the two lists; the things you should be doing against your reasons for not doing them. It will be impossible for you to reconcile the two if the things you should be doing are really important. You'll want to stop procrastinating and start getting things done as soon as you recognize this.

Now, go through this section and look at all the suggestions that are offered. Some of them deal with you and the way you behave. Others relate more to situations you can find yourself in. Decide which ones can help you most and get started with those right away. Come back to the others as your confidence builds. Add to the list whenever you can. And be sure to plan your work to avoid going off in a dozen different directions. Keep up your enthusiasm even when you encounter difficulties. Accept mistakes if you make them and keep trying to do better.

The first suggestion is probably the key to all the rest. Take a look at it now. It should help you with everything you do.

BE HAPPY

The way you feel about what you have to do will greatly affect the way you do it. If you're happy you'll be done sooner, have fewer problems, and enjoy the happiness of other people. On the other hand, if you're angry or dissatisfied, your work will drag on, you'll make mistakes, and the people around you will go out of their way to avoid you.

Abraham Lincoln said "You're about as happy as you make up your mind to be." You might have to work at it, but you can start by thinking happy thoughts. Put fear, anger, and frustration out of your mind. Be happy toward other people. Look for happy things in your environment. Read happy books, go to happy movies, and laugh at things you think are funny. You'll stop procrastinating a lot faster if you can get in the habit of being happy.

Develop a happy, healthy attitude and go to work on all the things you've been putting off. Do it now. You'll find your enthusiasm and happiness will be contagious to others.

As you get started it would help you a lot to run alongside so you can get a good look at yourself.

KNOW YOURSELF

Take time to find out why you're bothered by procrastination. Think about your capabilities and limitations and the levels of achievement that are open to you. Examine your goals and objectives to see if they're really attainable. Recall your history of successes and failures. Try to see what lies in the future. Compare yourself to others, especially if you're evaluated in competitive situations. Clarify your self-image and get to know who you are.

Learn to recognize and understand your moods. They're conscious states of mind in which emotions gain control of your behavior. Make them work for you, not against you. You might have to change a mood before starting to work on a task, especially if it causes you to procrastinate. But first you have to know what kind of mood you're in.

A small part of a complex task might fit your present mood. So go to work on it. Tackle the hard parts of your task as you get into more productive moods. Just be careful. If you're overly concerned about your moods, you could spend all your time trying to control your emotions without getting anything done.

Keep a diary. You'll be able to change your behavior much easier if you know what you've been doing. Record your moods and emotions. Know the ones that help you as well as the ones that make you procrastinate. You'll get a better perspective of who you are if you keep a good record and study it often. You'll be able to emphasize your strengths and supress your weaknesses.

As you learn more about yourself you'll probably discover some things you're afraid of. Those fears can cause you to procrastinate unless you learn how to overcome them.

CONQUER YOUR FEARS

You have to deal directly with whatever you're afraid of if it makes you procrastinate. Write down everything you think will go wrong with a task if all your fears came true. Then write down how you would handle each problem as if it was the only thing you had to worry about. Your fears will quickly evaporate if you can discipline yourself to do this little exercise.

Fears live in the dark corners and hidden recesses of your mind. But they wither and die when you drag them out into the open and meet them head-on.

Dale Carnegie, in his book *How to Stop Worrying and Start Living*, suggested a formula for solving worry situations. Here it is.

1. Ask yourself what's the worst that can possibly happen.
2. Write down precisely what you're worrying about.
3. Prepare to accept the worst if you have to.
4. Write down as many solutions to your problem as you can think of.
5. Decide on the best solution.
6. Start immediately to carry out that decision.
7. Calmly proceed to improve on what you see as the worst.

The words of Thomas Carlyle are also helpful for conquering

your fears. "Our main business is not to see what lies dimly at a distance, but to do what lies clearly at hand."

Your mind has to be ready whenever you set out to conquer fear, or anything else for that matter. That means you should be doing some mental gymnastics to keep your mind alert and active.

EXERCISE YOUR MIND

You should exercise your mind every day. Over time you'll develop some very good habits that will lead you out of the rut of procrastination and into a full and rewarding life. Here are some mental exercises you should try as often as you can.

Contemplate: Concentrate on spiritual things as a form of private devotion. Take time to smell the flowers, witness the sunrise and sunset, and enjoy sights, sounds, and smells. Consume the pleasures of your senses.

Study: Learn something new every day.

Reflect: Think about the events of the past. They give fullness to the present and the future.

Initiate Action: Do something that requires initiative and imagination on your part.

Achieve: Bring closure to some task or some aspect of your life, especially something you've been neglecting.

Create: Give something to the world that will last beyond your lifetime.

These exercises will not only keep you on your toes, but they'll also help you accomplish tasks you might previously have thought were impossible.

You have to involve more than just your mind if you're going to stop procrastinating. You also have to involve all five of your senses.

STIMULATE YOUR SENSES

You probably aren't going to procrastinate if you're really involved in a task. And one way to get involved is to utilize all five of your senses each time you start to work. This is especially true when you try to see yourself doing a task. It's also true when you try to break your task down into smaller subtasks.

You can imagine in your mind's eye a fall football game if you can recall the smell of grass on the playing field, see the beautiful fall leaves, taste hot dogs and coffee, and hear the sounds of the crowd and the marching bands.

Your ability to recall sensory stimuli is limited only by your imagination. So approach each task with all of your senses. Taste it, smell it, see it, hear it, and touch it. You'll have a much easier time completing a task if you can create a vivid image of it or of the things related to it.

After you get your senses involved, go down deep and get at the real you. And be nice to yourself because you're a very good person.

BOOST YOUR EGO

You might procrastinate because you lack motivation, are depressed, or feel sorry for yourself. If that's true, you need to build yourself up and improve your self-image. Take time out from your task, give yourself a pep talk, and tell yourself why you're a good and capable person. Acknowledge your strengths where they exist. But set aside your weaknesses for now because everybody has more than enough of those to worry about.

Boosting your ego will improve your self-confidence and restore your enthusiasm. And you'll get a lot more done as long as you truly believe in yourself.

Keep a file folder of positive motivators. You can include inspirational messages or recognitions and awards you've won. Humor has tremendous therapeutic effects so be sure you include cartoons, anecdotes, or other funny things that make you laugh. Use anything that will keep you in good spirits and give you the confidence you need to reach your objectives.

Sometimes you can give your ego a tremendous boost by paying recognition to all the good things you do.

REWARD YOURSELF

A simple reward system can help you stop procrastinating, especially if you're faced with several difficult tasks. Start by assigning points to the things you have to do. The hard tasks should earn you more points than the easy ones. Bonus points can be given for exceeding your own standards. Then choose rewards you'd like to have.

A hot-fudge sundae can be an excellent reward for adhering to a rigorous program of diet and exercise. A bottle of good wine, a night at the movies, or sleeping late can all be used as effective rewards if you enjoy them.

Your rewards can be simple and inexpensive. But they should be things that are important to you. Gold stars pasted on a progress chart can provide the lift needed to keep you going after you've reached important milestones in your task. Try different things until you can identify a system of rewards that will help you stop procrastinating. You'll soon be experiencing a whole new array of accomplishments.

Be sure to remember two things. Reward yourself only when you earn it. And when you earn a reward, be sure to take it. A reward system will only work if you strictly adhere to it.

Reward systems are particularly effective when you have to change or eliminate some major aspect of your behavior like a useless habit.

CHANGE YOUR HABITS

Sometimes you have to eliminate a habit or change some pattern of behavior before you can stop procrastinating. You might have to give up the coffee breaks you take every morning and afternoon, especially if they're ill-timed or serve no useful purpose. Or you might have to give up TV programs you watch religiously, even though they no longer stimulate, interest, or amuse you. You'll have lots more time for completing important tasks if you can eliminate your unproductive habits.

It's easier to change or eliminate a habit if you reward yourself for doing so. That's because reward is far more effective than punishment or indifference when you're trying to change your behavior. So reward yourself for taking the initiative and starting something even if you later get discouraged and quit. You'll feel a lot better than if you punished yourself for quitting. You may be able to bring about a significant and positive change in your habits if you just keep at it.

Of all the habits you have, the one you want to break right away is the habit of procrastinating. A good attitude will give you the momentum you need to make the changes you want. But you also need to understand what it is you're trying to accomplish.

ANALYZE

Try to thoroughly analyze everything you have to do. It's easy and the results are usually pretty effective.

Take a sheet of paper and draw a line down the middle. On one side list all the reasons you have for finishing a task. On the other side, list all the reasons you have for postponing it. Be sure to include everything you can think of. Then compare the two lists when you're done.

You'll come up with more reasons for doing a task than for delaying it if it's really important. And just putting those reasons down on paper should give you the motivation you need to get started.

If you should happen to come up with lots of reasons for delaying a task, drop it and go on to something else. It's crazy for you to keep working on something that causes anxiety and frustration and makes you procrastinate. Get rid of it unless there's a real good reason for hanging on to it.

If someone else has assigned a task to you, you'd better do it even though you'd like to postpone it. But if you find it impossible to do, you may have to withdraw from the position you're in. That could mean quitting your job or ending a personal relationship. You'll know what to do if you've carefully analyzed your task. And you'll find the correct choice fairly easy to make.

Once you've learned to analyze your task, study it closely. Because it will be a lot easier for you to finish it if you know more about it.

STUDY YOUR TASK

Lack of knowledge causes apathy. And apathy is a forerunner of procrastination. You can conquer both by learning more about the things you have to do.

Get involved with your task. If it's worth doing, it's worth knowing about. Do some research if you're uncertain about your facts. The search for more information can serve as a leading task. And it will provide the momentum you need to get off to a good start. Your interest will increase as you learn more. And you'll be able to finish your task easier and quicker by applying your new knowledge. Share your knowledge with others and involve them in your task. They'll not only absorb your enthusiasm, they'll also support you in your efforts.

Charles Kettering said "A problem well-stated is a problem half-solved." Learning as much as you can about a task and developing an interest in it is half the battle of getting it done.

Sometimes it's harder to tackle large, complex tasks. But there's a way to whittle them down to size so you can handle them very easily.

SUBDIVIDE

If you think your task is complicated, subdivide it. Dissect it as much as possible until you can clearly see how it's put together. You'll get a lot more done if you can take it piece by piece.

It'll only take you a few minutes to complete each subtask if you've done a thorough job of subdividing. You'll find the whole task can be done much quicker than you expected. You'll also discover that your task will probably be a lot less complicated than you first thought.

The enthusiasm you'll experience in going through the subtasks will speed you toward your goal and give you a great sense of accomplishment. But if you come to a dead end along the way, stop! Work on another subtask until the hurdle clears. Thinking about and completing something else will give your mind a refreshing break. When you come back to your problem, you'll probably have a solution that would have been lost if you'd sat still and worried about it.

Subdividing is particularly effective for unpleasant tasks. Almost anyone can do something they dislike if they only have to do it for a short time. So break the tough ones down into small subtasks. Spread them out and fill in the time between with things you like to do. It may take a little longer, but you'll feel a lot better when you're done.

Identifying subtasks without doing any is busywork. It's just another form of procrastination. So develop a specific plan for completing all the parts once you've identified them. Because you'll come to a dead end awfully quick if you don't know where you're going.

ORGANIZE AND PLAN

The best way to stop procrastinating is to never start in the first place. You can do this by planning; something lots of people talk about but few actually carry out.

Start by setting some long-term goals and objectives. A goal is an idealistic, hoped-for accomplishment that can be done almost anytime. It's a general statement from which specific objectives can be developed. Trying to lose an unspecified amount of weight is an example of a goal.

An objective is a clear statement of something you want to do in a specified time period. An example would be your desire to start today to lose seven pounds within a three-week period. A good objective is quantifiable. Then you know for sure if you've reached it.

Plan every day. As the first thing in the morning or the last thing the night before, make a checklist of everything you need to do to accomplish your goals and objectives. Set priorities for your tasks so you're sure of doing the important things first.

Take time to reflect at the end of each day. Look at your list of tasks and see how well you did. Incorporate your insights about today into your plans for tomorrow. Fill in extra time with special tasks. Spread your tasks over a longer time period if you're short on time during any one day. Try to do better each day. And build a sense of improvement into your expectations.

Be aware of the dangers of planning. John Gardner, in his book *Self-Renewal*, cautioned against being overwhelmed by the process of planning when he said ". . . the concern for 'how it is done' is also one of the diseases on which societies die. Little by little, preoccupation with method, technique, and procedure gains a subtle dominance over the whole process of goal seeking. How it is done becomes more important than whether it is done."

As Gardner saw it, you can get trapped in the process. Then suddenly you lose sight of your goals and objectives.

Be goal oriented. Focus on your objectives and move briskly toward their completion. Take shortcuts when you see them. Throw away any incidental tasks that get in your way. Think about getting things done, not just doing things.

It's a common fact. The more time you spend in planning, the less time you'll need for completing a task. Because a task well-defined is a task half done.

Be sure you know which tasks should be done before others. Because the order you select will greatly affect your ability to carry out your plan.

SET PRIORITIES

You should always do the most important things first. You can start by arranging all your tasks in order of priority. Just be careful how you do this.

Edwin Bliss, in his book *Getting Things Done: The ABC's of Time Management*, provides some excellent guidelines for establishing priorities. Here are the categories he suggests you use.

1. *Important and Urgent.* These tasks belong at the top of your list. You've got to do them right away or you'll suffer serious consequences.
2. *Important But Not Urgent.* These tasks should be near the top. But lots of people ignore them because they can be postponed. They include things like getting a physical examina-

tion, writing a letter to a friend, or saying, "I love you."
3. *Urgent But Not Important.* These tasks tend to be high on other people's lists. If you put them ahead of your important tasks, you're probably looking for approval from others.
4. *Busy Work.* These tasks can provide a welcome relief from difficult tasks if you control them. But spending too much time on them is just another form of procrastination.
5. *Wasted Time.* This group of tasks should be excluded from your list of priorities. When you consider things that waste time, it's good to remember the words of Sarah Doudney. "Oh the wasted hours of life that have drifted by! Oh, the good that might have been, lost without a sigh."

Feel free to change priorities once you begin to work on your tasks. Reexamine them from time to time so you always know what should come first. Be determined to say "no" to tasks that can be disruptive. Keep your goals and objectives in front of you. And do what's necessary to get them done.

Some people have a hard time taking the first step in completing a task. As a matter-of-fact they need help taking steps of any kind.

BE DECISIVE

Start working on a task as soon as you have everything you need. You can make adjustments as you go. The worst thing you can do is sit in the starting blocks and procrastinate. Get moving if you have all the facts you need. Forget about the contingencies that might occur. If you discover later you've made a mistake, admit it and start over.

Get rid of a task if it looks impossible or if you'd rather do something else. Scratch it from your list of things to do. You'll create lots of unnecessary anxiety if you hang on to something that should be discarded.

Deciding to accept or reject a task is sometimes difficult. But prolonging that decision is just another form of procrastination. So come to terms with your task. Make your decision to go ahead or leave it alone. Whatever you decide, you'll at least avoid the anxiety and indecision that would come from continued procrastination.

You can ensure that something will get done if you do more than just make up your mind to do it. Sometimes it takes just a little added touch to firm up your decision.

MAKE A COMMITMENT

Any important task has a greater chance of being completed when you formally commit yourself to doing it. Your commitment can be a promise to reach a specific objective like losing ten pounds, giving up cigarettes, or writing a book. And you'll be more likely to keep a public commitment made to someone else—a spouse, friend, or employer—than if you made it to yourself.

You should make your commitments to people you trust and respect. They can get involved in your efforts by reviewing your progress toward a goal, helping you set deadlines, or evaluating your results.

You naturally start thinking more about other people and less about your own self-interests when you make a commitment to someone else. Your concerns, fears, and anxieties become secondary to the expectations of people you feel good about. This attitude change will help significantly to break your habit of procrastination. And having others share in your accomplishments will make it all a lot more enjoyable.

Making a commitment to finish a task can help you get it done. But sometimes you need a little more help in getting it started.

LAUNCH A LEADING TASK

The first step you take to stop procrastinating is often the most important one. It can also be the easiest if it's a leading task.

A leading task should take you right into a larger task that you've been postponing. It should be relatively simple and require very little planning or conscious effort on your part. In can break the shackles of inertia and launch you toward your goal if it's a good leading task.

A leading task can be as simple as sharpening your pencil or looking up the phone number of someone you should call. The purchase of a jogging suit can start you off on an exercise program. Getting a calorie counter can be the first step in going on a diet. You can even start writing a report just by clearing your desk.

Remember the old saying "The journey of a thousand miles begins with a single step." Make your first step a leading task. It'll help you stop procrastinating.

You'll be able to keep up with your tasks if you know where you're going. You'll do even better if you can look to the future and see what lies ahead.

VISUALIZE COMPLETION

You can do any task faster and better if you can see yourself getting it done. The key lies in the intensity of your vision and the depth of your concentration. You can develop this technique through the practice of a simple exercise.

Go into a small room, close the door, and sit down in a comfortable chair, couch, or recliner. Close your eyes, relax completely, put all distracting thoughts out of your mind, and concentrate very hard on having the door open again. Picture the open door in your mind's eye. Imagine your hand on the knob, turning it and opening the door. Concentrate very hard for several minutes until you can clearly see the door being opened. Keep all distracting thoughts from interfering with your concentration. Then open your eyes, stand up, and look right at the door.

If you've concentrated very hard, and if you're like most people, you'll want to open the door. The picture you formed in your mind's eye will motivate you to act right away. And you'll probably feel very uncomfortable if the door stays closed. You'll stop procrastinating very soon if you can concentrate like this with all your tasks. Because if you can see something being done, you'll be motivated to do it.

Reaching a deep level of concentration depends on your ability to relax and clear your mind of distracting thoughts. You can acquire this skill by practicing the "relaxation response" that was developed by Dr. Herbert Benson, Associate Professor of Medicine at Harvard University Medical School. It's like many other meditation techniques and follows a standard procedure.

Start by lying or sitting in a comfortable position with your eyes closed. Allow all your muscles to relax, beginning with your toes and working up to your facial muscles. Breathe easily and naturally through your nose. As you breath out, silently repeat a word or phrase to help keep your mind from wandering to distracting thoughts. You'll soon be able to bring about the relaxation response with very little effort if you practice every day.

When you're fully relaxed, think of completing a task and concentrate only on that. Make a habit of seeing yourself doing things you might otherwise postpone. You'll soon discover you're getting a lot more done with no procrastination.

Sometimes you may be too close to your task to see it being completed. Just stand back and take a detatched look. Or get someone to help you. They may see a solution that you've missed.

Consider every aspect of your task without taking anything for granted. Try this. Sketch a telephone dial with all the holes, numbers, and letters. Or lay out the buttons on a pushbutton phone. You probably use a phone several times a day so this should be relatively easy. But this little exercise will be very difficult if you've taken your phone for granted. This is true for any task when you lose your perspective and have difficulty seeing it completed.

The amount of time that's available for doing a task often determines if it's difficult or not. That's why it's so important to know how to utilize the time you have.

APPRECIATE TIME

Some of your tasks have to be done on certain dates like birthdays and anniversaries. And you'll miss them if you procrastinate. Other tasks, like starting a diet, can be done almost any time.

You have to know what your deadlines are and how to work with them. Learn to budget time as you would any valuable resource. Samuel Smiles knew the value of time when he said "Lost wealth may be replaced by industry, lost knowledge by study, lost health by temperance or medicine. But lost time is gone forever."

Identify activities that waste time. Ask yourself if it would make any difference if you took time to goof off. You'll know you wasted time if afterwards you feel bad about postponing something you should have done.

Try to fill in soft spots where you might otherwise waste time. Write a note to yourself or to someone to whom you owe a letter if you find yourself waiting for something to happen. You'd be surprised at the number of times in a day you can complete simple but otherwise forgotten tasks. You can also use these little tidbits of time for meditation and relaxation.

Take a few minutes every morning to schedule your day. Life is pretty imprecise so you shouldn't try to schedule every minute. If you're too exact, you'll get frustrated by all the distractions that are bound to occur. Keep a diary so you can see how you spent the time that was available.

Parkinson's Law says work will expand to fill the time available for its completion. Conversely, you'll probably get rid of lots of useless activity and wasted effort if you make less time available for doing things. Know your deadlines. And keep a tight schedule that prevents dawdling and procrastination. Acknowledge success along the way so you can keep going at a steady pace.

Unfortunately there may still be times when you feel like your task has gotten the best of you. That's when you should look to other people for help.

DELEGATE

If you're overwhelmed by a complex task, you can avoid procrastinating by delegating some of your load to other people.

Start by carefully dividing your task into clearly defined parts. Make sure the people you've delegated to understand the interrelationships of the subtasks. They may end up procrastinating like you did if they're confused. Then you'll get back more work than you gave out. But if you give them lots of information at the beginning, they won't have to keep coming back to you for clarification.

Once you've delegated full responsibility for certain subtasks you'll be free to go to work on what you kept. As others complete their assignments, you can gather their results together with your own into a final product. You'll be surprised at the ease with which you can bring it all to completion. And you'll make other people happy by letting them make significant contributions.

Involving other people in your task can sometimes be difficult. But there's one thing you can do that will minimize your problems.

BE IMPARTIAL

You should always be aware of the influence other people have on what you do. Because you'll procrastinate and cause a lot of unnecessary anxiety if you let individual personalities keep you from completing your tasks.

Be tactful and considerate of the opinions of others. Treat everyone equally and try to keep them happy. If you have a very important task to do, you'll have to do it in spite of the possibility of personality conflicts. Come to terms with your potential adversaries. Your worries may be unfounded. But if conflicts remain, diffuse them before your work begins. And if all else fails, you'll just have to go ahead in the face of criticism from others.

You're letting other people control your life if their feelings make you procrastinate. This will not only cause you a lot of anxiety, but it'll also keep you from reaching your goals and objectives. It's your life to live. You have to do it the best way you can without letting others interfere.

Your life can also be controlled by the things that surround you. So to keep from procrastinating, you have to recognize and understand all the forces that can get in your way.

REGULATE YOUR ENVIRONMENT

Your environment can cause you to procrastinate if everything isn't the way you want it. The lighting may be poor. You may be too hot or too cold. Or it may be too noisy. All of these distractions can cause you to delay or postpone important tasks.

So determine what kind of environment is best for you. Experiment with different levels of noise and light intensity. Work alone or with others. Work early in the day, late at night, or at midday. Work right before or after strenuous exercise. Keep track of your results. And identify optimum times and conditions when you're at your best.

Create a realistic environment, one that's best for you. Make changes as they're needed. Strive for an environment that will motivate you to act. And feel free to try new approaches if they can keep you from procrastinating.

In addition to changing your environment, you should also control the way in which you do your work.

SEEK DIVERSIONS

When you've worked very hard on a task you sometimes get bored or fatigued. That's when you procrastinate instead of completing a task or starting a new one. At that point it's a good idea to take a break and seek a diversion.

You should always create a stopping point or milestone before you leave a task. Finish everything you can up to that point. Then when you come back to your task you'll know exactly where you left off.

Physical activity—especially walking—is very effective as a diversion. If you've reached a milestone in your task and you find it hard to continue, stop and go for a walk. The exercise will clear your mind and stimulate your heart. The sights and sounds you'll encounter will help generate new ideas. And you'll gain a new burst of energy that will help you finish your task.

When you're experiencing physical fatigue, take a rest. A short catnap will help restore bodily processes. And it'll allow your subconscious thoughts to incubate, providing you with new solutions to existing problems.

This is the last of the suggestions. Hopefully, as you went through them, others came to mind and you wrote them down. If you did, you should have a long list of things that will help you stop procrastinating. Now it's time to take the third and fourth steps in the method that was introduced to you at the beginning of this book. You've got to put your plan into action.

YOUR PLAN OF ACTION

You've taken some awfully big steps since you started this journey. You've learned why most people procrastinate. And you have a much better idea of why you do it. You've read about lots of things you can do to stop procrastinating. Some of them you already knew about, some were new to you, and others came to mind as you went along.

Now you have to sift through it all and come up with a plan of action. It has to be right for you, serving your needs and meeting your capabilities and limitations. It should contain bits and pieces of everything you've read and learned about. It should guide you in deciding what has to be done and when and how you should do it. Then once you have your plan of action, you have to apply it.

Picture in your mind's eye all your essential goals and objectives. Then with this book at your side, take off, move out, set sail, break camp, make tracks. Start doing all the important things that are out there waiting for you. Stay with your plan and recognize your achievements. Savor the excitment of growth and development. And relish the happiness that will surely come.

STOP PROCRASTINATING—DO IT!

BIBLIOGRAPHY

Benson, Dr. Herbert. *The Relaxation Response.* New York: William Morrow and Company, Inc., 1975.

Benzaia, Diana. "Procrastination: Your Biggest Hangup." *Harper's Bazaar.* February, 1979, pp. 60, 147.

Bliss, Edwin C. *Getting Things Done: The ABC's of Time Management.* New York: Bantam Books, Inc., 1976.

Carnegie, Dale. *How to Stop Worrying and Start Living.* New York: Simon and Schuster, 1948.

Douglass, Merrill E. "How to Conquer Procrastination." (Audio Cassette) Grandville, Michigan: Time Management Center, 1975.

Dyer, Dr. Wayne W. *Your Erroneous Zones.* New York: Funk & Wagnalls, 1976.

Ellis, Albert and Knaus, William J. *Overcoming Procrastination.* New York: New American Library, 1977.

Fein, Elaine. "Stop Procrastinating." *Seventeen,* January, 1979, p. 37.

Friedman, Meyer and Rosenman, Ray. *Type A Behavior and Your Heart.* New York: Fawcett Crest Books, 1974.

Gardner, John W. *Self Renewal: The Individual and the Innovative Society.* New York: Harper & Row, Publishers, Inc., 1963.

Krenis, Lee. "Behavior Modification: The New Therapy." *Harper's Bazaar,* January, 1979, pp. 111, 129-130.

Lindstrom, Jane. "How Will You Know Unless I Tell You?" *Reader's Digest,* April, 1977, pp. 43, 44, 46.

Newsline. "The Exercise Dropout Test." *Psychology Today*, August, 1979, pp. 25-26.

Strong, S.R., Wambach, C.A., Lopez, F.G., and Cooper, R.K. "Motivational and Equipping Functions of Interpretation in Counseling." *Journal of Counseling Psychology*, 1979, pp. 98-107.

Wheeler, David R. "Behavior Modification for Writers." *The Writer*, June, 1979, pp. 19-20.

Ziesat, Harold A., Rosenthal, Ted L., and White, Glen M. "Behavioral Self-control in Treating Procrastination of Studying." *Psychological Reports*, 1978, pp. 59-69.

INDEX

CATALOG OF CURRENT BOOKS

NOW AVAILABLE

Pathway Books

700 Parkview Terrace
Golden Valley, Minnesota 55416
(612) 377-1521

ORDER FORM

□ **NOW TO OVERCOME A BAD BACK** **$5.95**
A steady favorite among bad-back sufferers and doctors all over the country. It's already sold in eight foreign countries and has become the bible of back pain for millions.

□ **REJECTION** **$3.95**
A great book for the person who's trying to survive rejection and promote acceptance. It's bound to be a bestseller for sales-people, jobseekers, and lovers. It hits at the heart of the leading cause of anxiety and depression.

□ **STOP PROCRASTINATING—DO IT!** **$2.25**
Now in its eleventh printing and selling better than ever following an NBC TODAY show appearance. A perfect book for busy executives, harried homemakers, active college students, or anyone else who wants to get more out of life.

□ **GET SET . . . GO!** **$2.95**
An extremely useful book with clear, easy to understand guidelines that will help you plan your future and gain control of your destiny.

□ **MIDDLE AGE IS NOT A DISEASE** **$3.95**
This delightful book, with its amazing facts and rib-tickling humor, is the perfect gift for anyone who has hurdled the 40's barrier and is trying to cope with the mental and physical disruptions of middle age.

□ **ESCAPE TO THE GUNFLINT** **$3.95**
A thrilling suspense novel that takes place in the Twin Cities and north woods of Minnesota. It's an exciting page turner that can't be put down until it's finished.

ORDER YOUR BOOKS NOW!
Every order is filled the day it's received. Send check or money order — no cash or c.o.d. — along with .85¢ per copy to cover postage and handling. MN residents add 6% sales tax.

Name _____

Address _____

City _____

State/Zip _____

☐ PLEASE PUT MY NAME ON YOUR MAILING LIST